THE BURTON & ASHBY LIGHT RAILWAY

(and adjacent lines)

BY
C.T. GOODE

Car No. 2 asks everyone to 'Remember the lifeboat demonstration' as it takes the corner at the foot of Bearwood Hill. No. 3 is close behind it as a Burton car goes away uphill.   National Railway Museum

ISBN 1870313 15 1
72 Woodland Drive, Anlaby, Hull. HU10 7HX

Produced by
Burstwick Print & Publicity Services
Hull.

Contents

Early railways West of Leicester	P. 5
Swadlincote is linked to the system	P. 7
Early days: light railway proposals	P. 9
Construction begins	P.12
Opening day and a run on the line	P.16
Ashby as a town	P.26
The branch to Gresley	P.28
B & A operation and services	P.29
The staff	P.33
Trials and Tribulations	P.36
Rail services on the major local lines	P.39
Ill-met by Gresley station	P.43

Abbreviations.

SO	Saturdays only.
MR	Midland Railway.
NS	North Staffs. Railway.
SW	Saturdays excepted.
LNWR	London & North Western Railway.
1 chain	22 yards.
10 chains	1 furlong.
8 furlongs	1 mile.
12 pence	1 shilling. (5 present day pence)
20 shillings	£1

Foreword

The Burton & Ashby Light Railway makes an attractive subject about which to write, being an unusual offshoot of a great railway company and having about it the aura and tradition, as well as the striking livery. The line is also something of a puzzle in that it was in competition with the local railway system, especially at Gresley, and thus with its own interests, though purists would argue that the passengers gained for the B & A in its early days were chiefly local ones who had little to gain from an infrequent train service in any case.

I have drawn heavily on three earlier works of varying degrees of merit. The first is 'An English Country Tramway' by R. B. Parr, a small book published in 1970 and a write-up of one of his lectures of 1948; then a useful scissors and paste book 'Sixpenny Switchback' by Messrs. White and Storer which is a collection of photographs with much local information which I now acknowledge with thanks. Lastly and most recently, there is a collection of old postcards of the trams in 'The Burton & Ashby Light Railways' by M. Bown, published in 1991 as part of a local history series which conveys the atmosphere of the line very well. There had initially been difficulty in obtaining copies of photographs for use in this new work, after seeing so many in print previously; however, I am grateful to Mr. C. Adcock for the loan of his late father-in-law's collection (a former B & A driver) to copy and to the National Railway Museum, York for unearthing the original negatives in their collection.

Thanks, too, to the National Library of Scotland for assistance in producing large scale maps showing the course of the line, to the staff of Coalville library for pointing me in the right direction in the early stages, and to Don. Steggles of Newton Abbot library for help with the railway timetables.

C. Tony Goode.
Anlaby, Hull.
March. 1994.

Early days West of Leicester

The first railways, or plate ways as they were more often called, came about in a particular district, firstly became of the need for the carriage of coal to a canal or to some local centre of population, this being by far the main priority for folk who, not needing to travel far themselves or to transport their livestock, nevertheless welcomed a readily available source of heat for their comfort and energy for budding local industries.

So it was in the case of Leicester, whose coal arrived at first by canal from the Nottinghamshire coalfield, leaving the Leicester owners to transport their produce along the inadequate roads. Canals were slow but at least cheap and consistent, whereas roads on which the heavy carts ran were slower still and most unreliable in bad weather. A local man, William Stenson, owner of Long Lane pit, happened to pay a visit to the north in 1827 and was impressed by the famed Stockton & Darlington Railway at work. On his return he discussed the new method of propulsion with John Ellis, a Quaker businessman who happened to be a friend of George Stephenson and who stated that he would be delighted to raise the subject of a new railway with him. This involved his travelling to see Stephenson at Rainhill cutting on the newly built Liverpool & Manchester Railway, and together the two men studied the map of the terrain where the coal mines were situated in Leicestershire. Both George and his son, Robert Stephenson returned with Ellis to Leicester and, in due course, at a meeting held at the Bell Hotel in that town, a committee was formed to float the new Leicester & Swannington Railway, this on 12th. February 1829, with Robert as Engineer. The line obtained its Act on 30th. May 1830, shortly before the Liverpool & Manchester was opened.

Construction was based on the same gradient principles as the canals, levels, then ups and downs, with two cable worked inclines, one up at 1 in 29 to Swannington, and one down at 1 in 17 to Swannington served by a stationary engine. There was also a tunnel of 1 mile 36 yd. at Glenfield, always a 'Must' for thrilling the early passengers.

The little line, of 16 miles opened officially on 14th. July 1832 and ran from a terminus by the river Soar at Leicester West Bridge. 'Comet', a little 0-4-2 which had been shipped by water from the Forth works at Newcastle to Hull, then by canal to Leicester, was made ready and, with steam up set off with two blue painted four wheel coaches, the only ones available, and some plain wagons for the plebs, contriving to reduce the height of her chimney somewhat by contact with the aforementioned tunnel. Coal traffic was immense after adoption by the Midland Railway. The line eventually found itself with some superior 6 wheeler coaches after 1887. The final tally of earlier locomotives used on the line was ten.

The Midland Railway was formed on 10th. May 1844 by the amalgamation of the North Midland, Midland Counties and Birmingham & Derby Jc. Railways, and in August 1845 the little Leicester & Swannington was gobbled up.

The Grecian front of Ashby station, designed originally by R. Chaplyn and now used as offices *The Midland Railway Trust*

On 23rd. March 1848 a line was opened from Leicester's main MR station at Campbell St. to Burton-on-Trent, a distance of 31 miles, which ran to Desford where it joined the L & S line from West Bridge and ran on through Coalville and Ashby with a diversion from the old inclines near Bagworth. Leicester itself had first of all been linked to London via the Midland Counties line to Rugby, opened on 1st. July 1840, and later by the line of 8th. May 1857 opened through Bedford to Hitchin. The direct St. Pancras route was to come after 13th. July 1868.

The line to Burton ran its course from east to west across the southern part of Ashby-de-la-Zouch, providing a fine station building, while beyond it, on the north side was the platform of the same company's line to Derby which was a hybrid mixture of ideas. The MR had brought the Ashby canal in 1846 and had found itself with the Ticknall tramway, so used the land made available to provide a standard gauge line which would join the existing goods line from Breedon to Pear Tree on the main line to the south west out of Derby. An Act was passed for this on 5th. July 1865. The line had a passenger service from 1st. January 1874 to 22nd. September 1930 (see page 42). The opening was in easy stages with basic station premises; closure was as fragmented. During the 1939-45 war the WD occupied the line from Ashby Smisby road to Melbourne, closing to Lount in 1945, to Worthington in 1968, Chellaston East Jc. in 1981 and to Pear Tree from West Jc. in 1973. The line was reopened to passengers from Pear Tree to Sinfin on 4th. October 1976.

The London & North Western Railway were looking longingly at the Leicestershire coalfield and had already skirted this by means of their South Leics. line running from Nuneaton to Wigston, of 1864. The MR were, of course, safely ensconced and had in fact prepared their own blocking proposal to thwart any LNW aims in this direction; the enthusiasm vanished, however, once an outlet to Burton was assured to the interloper. The lion and the lamb lay down together and a joint committee of the two companies proposed a jointly run line to run from Nuneaton to Ashby and Coalville. Initially the LNW worked from Nuneaton to Overseal station, just short of the Burton to Ashby line, that is, along the left hand fork of the junction at Shackerstone which lay out in the country some eight miles to the south. The company also ran trains along the right hand fork to its own station at Coalville (East). Post 1883 a purely LNW branch line was opened from here to Loughborough, ten miles distant and somewhat far-flung for the LNWR, along which local workings ran to and from Shackerstone. From 1st. July 1890 the LNW was able to run through to Burton and Ashby by way of a junction with the MR at Moira (Overseal) and operated four through services to Burton and a through coach to Buxton, as well as four trains to Ashby. The MR local services ran between Shackerstone and Coalville MR (Town) using a spur between that line and the company's own Burton line at Coalville. It will be gathered, then, that there was already much railway activity in the area west of Leicester before the turn of the century.

Swadlincote is linked to the system

The line to Burton took a fairly easy route to the west of higher ground which only impinged once in the shape of Gresley tunnel, of 400 yd., after which came the run down to Gresley station which was the only halt before Burton, $5^1/_4$ miles away. Gresley was in the early years the railhead for the nearby villages of Castle and Church Gresley, and also Swadlincote, which in 1861 numbered a mere 11,076 folk, whereas today's figure is 23,388, as over the years the place has become an agglomeration of small villages forming the whole community- Gresley, Newhall, Midway and Wooden Box, later known as the more decorous Woodville. Brick and the tile work, pipeworks and coal mines galore sprang up as a result of the older clay pits and, as it did so, the once beautiful countryside all but vanished. This transformation was helped by the MR who, on 3rd. August 1846 obtained an Act for a short branch to Swadlincote of 2 miles 31 ch from the Burton line, which had its first goods trains from 2nd. October 1848 and passenger trains on 1st. April 1859. This line probably did extend to Woodville by a little over a further mile, as the local trains were booked as running there through Swadlincote. However, a second short branch was opened from the Burton line at Swainspark, east of Gresley tunnel to Woodville where a goods terminus was situated. In due course the suggestion was made that the two lines should be linked, so that an Act was obtained on 29th. June 1875, with goods trains using what was now a large loop looking like a tinplate train set from 12th. April 1880, followed by passenger services from 1st. May 1883. The curves were tight, of No 1 radius if one wishes to

Above A leggy 2P No. 40396 and ancient tender enter Burton station from the north with heavy goods. *The Midland Railway Trust*

Below A heavy train leaves the north end of Burton station, helped by 'Compound' No. 41163 piloting a 'jubilee'. Notice the local service in the bay platform. *The Midland Railway Trust*

continue with the Hornby references, and with a couple of No. 1 tunnels, at Woodville (307 yd.) and Midway (104 yd.). The loop was single and dead straight as far as Swadlincote from the junction, with passing places, and the gradients were steep, though this did not prevent some main line trains from traversing the loop, especially at peak holiday times. The Woodville goods branch projected north east into the centre area of the loop to slightly beyond the junction of the Ashby and Burton roads, where the old terminus was, in later days, the Excelsior Pottery. The two thriving townships of Swadlincote and Woodville thus had their own train service, albeit a circuitous one, with six workings from Burton in 1910 for example, while the odd one out happened to be Newhall, a place of up to 9,000 people some distance to the west of Swadlincote, a fact which was in due course to play a major part in the promotion of the light railway in these parts. There was in fact a third branch line built out from the main line, a longish one up to Bretby colliery which passed near enough to the west of Newhall to have enabled a station to be sited on it; however, there is no evidence of any suggestion being made for such a facility, and the opportunity was allowed to pass.

Early days; light railway proposals

Obviously, then, something was required to link up more directly the growing centres of industry and attendant population, with Burton-on-Trent at 50,000, Swadlincote at 20,000 and a further 10,000 spread about an often quite hilly district for which a means of light railway traction would be very useful.

In 1899 a group of tramway promoters put forward a scheme, applying to Parliament for an Order to lay a line from Burton to Ashby, possibly at the time no more than a convenient place on the map to terminate, as traffic likely to be generated from that area east of Woodville would hardly match that from the rest of the system. The MR offered support for the scheme, but Burton-on-Trent corporation, which had recently started to run its own tram cars objected and the idea was withdrawn since it stood no chance of adoption once a local authority was against it. In 1900 a second attempt was made to provide a light railway by an interested group supported by Sir Bache Cunard, who was mostly likely a MR Director with a seat at Shantock Hall in Herts. For variety, this idea was supported by Burton corporation and the other interested local authorities, but opposed by the MR who, rather belatedly, feared competition against their railways in the area. The promoters were more single-minded on this occasion in their determination to secure a new line and eventually reached an agreement with the MR who stated that they would obtain powers to construct the railway. The MR proposed an Order of their own in May 1902, which was virtually similar to the one which to which they had objected before, the difference being that someone had obviously had the forethought to divert the line from the main road over half a mile of reserved track from the Stanhope Arms at Bretby through Newhall village

Ex MR Class Brewery tank No.. 41516 at Burton. October 1955
Photo Frank Ashley

which would otherwise have been isolated from a new means of transport. Burton seemed happy with arrangements, through the residents along Ashby road, directly east of the river bridge objected to having a new tramway running past their villas. The result was that the new line turned left on Corporation tracks along the Winshill route, leaving it in due course to run along High Bank road and regain the Ashby road. Swadlincote Urban District Council also had objections, along with other parties. On 27th. July 1903 they appealed against the Order, complaining that the trams would interfere with the market on Saturday evenings, a peculiar and unusual time, at which up to 2,000 people would gather, and feared annihilation of their market, due to trams passing through Market Place. It would eventually dawn that the cars would in fact bring in more customers from outlying areas that it would deter. The council also objected to the roads being laid with setts flanking a smoother surface in which the rails would be embedded, fearing that they would be difficult to maintain. The Surveyor to Swadlincote council also gave interesting figures he had collected on 16th. October 1902, a day on which 523 drays passed in the High street, with 593 on the next day, both tallies between 6 am and 8 pm and excluding various steam vehicles. The MR spokesman estimated this to be about 25 vehicles hourly each way, a fact which did not appear excessive. The reserved section of track proposed over the corner of

Gresley common was also jibbed at, a trifling objection as the land was waste in any event. The basic drawback of all street tramways, that the passage of trams along a busy roadway with frequent stops for passengers would halt other traffic hardly seems to have been mentioned at all. One objection by the Council did, however, require an Amendment to the Act, as we shall presently see.

There were four Railways in the original Act, this possibly giving rise to the occasional use of the plural in the system's title. No. 1 began at the junction of Stapenhill road and Newton road near the end of Burton corporation's Winshill route. Running over the latter's 3ft. 6in. lines in the town had been authorised in 1901, and the new line along High Bank road to the Ashby road was authorised originally for construction by Burton corporation but not proceeded with. Along this road the line went, then south at the Stanhope Arms over the fields to Sunnyside, Newhall and into Swadlincote across the railway by the station. Here was the setting of the further point of local dispute mentioned earlier, as the existing level crossing saw long delays with the gates closed for shunting movements. The local council pursued the matter and compelled the MR to build a bridge across, which that company was to maintain. From the centre of Swadlincote the line ran east through the town, terminating about 20 yd. north of the booking office at Ashby station, 8 miles, 5 furlongs, 9.5 chains in all.

Railway No. 2 was of 1 mile, 7 furlongs 3.6 chains from High street in Swadlincote at a junction with No. 1 southwards to Gresley common and along Church street to terminate at the north end of the road bridge over the MR at Gresley station. Railway No. 3 of just over 6 furlongs was to run from No. 1 on Woodville road, Swadlincote south west to joint No. 2 near School street, Gresley, thus forming east side of a large triangle. No. 4 was a slip of a line forming the south side of a triangle in Market Place, Swadlincote and linking Nos. 1 and 2. No. 3 did not survive long, and one wonders how much No. 4 was in fact used for running purposes.

The Bill was deposited in June 1902 and received Royal Assent on 5th. November, also authorised under a Light Railway Order of May 1902 with an Amendment for the railway bridge in 1906. The latter was signed by no less a person than David Lloyd George at the Board of Trade. Construction went on a pace against an estimated cost of £89,926.13s. 3d. Most of this went in the widening of narrow roads which were mainly unmetalled, a total of $4^1/_2$ miles out of $11^1/_2$ miles, with Leicestershire County Council empowered to widen to 24 ft. on the south side of the road, while Derbyshire could widen outside Swadlincote area only, and only there if absolutely necessary. Most drastic operations were in Ashby, where Bath street was widened on the west side and Derby street on the east, the MR seeing to the making good of kerbs and gulleys. Supporting posts for the overhead wires were to be illuminated, though this was apparently not carried out and no car nor any similar vehicle on the line was to exceed 6ft. 6 in. in width. Propulsion of the cars was to be either by animal or mechanical power, which left one wondering what was left, unless gravity or wind were in mind. Between the hours of 12 midnight and 5 am. the rails could be used by the relevant councils for the removal of night soil and other refuse, though this condition does not appear to have been taken up by anyone. Anyone repairing the roadway could also avail themselves of the facility. The Company was, if and as long as required by a local authority, to provide a waiting room for passengers on the route of the railway, to be approved by the local authority. There were, in fact, two of these, at Sunnyside and the road junctions in Woodville. After 35 years the local authorities had the option of purchasing the line, if the MR wished to sell it (Swadlincote wished this to be 25 years). In the shorter term, if the line were to be out of use for longer than three months, then it could be removed.

The bridge at Swadlincote was forced upon the company by the local council who were fearful of additional delays to traffic caused by the tramway, and it was provided under an Amendment Order of 1906, made of blue brick with a centre girder section, of 30 ft. width with pathways on each side.

Construction begins

Construction of the line began in several places under the direction of Charles H. Gadsby, the Engineer, in February 1905; at the Burton end it was originally planned to route the new line on private track up a steep incline between the Winshill and Stapenhill roads from Trent Bridge. This would have involved a gradient of 1 in 9, so the line went along the original Burton tram route by way of the easier 1 in 12 up Bearwood Hill. The corporation built a new line of 7 furlongs 5 chains from the junction of Bearwood Hill and High Bank roads and along the latter to the Ashby road, a section which, though owned by Burton-on-Trent, was never regularly used by them.

Some demolition of property was necessary in the High street in Newhall village, where it was hard to find a straight line of road and, in consequence, property was built askew in many cases.

The rails were of 90 lb. per yard, increasing to 95 lb. on curves, supplied by Walter Scott Ltd., laid on 6 in. concrete decked in granite. Points were 13 ft. 6 in long, of 60 ft. radius constructed by Edgar Allen & Co. or in some cases by Hadfield's, both of Sheffield. It is not clear, but points would most likely be changed by the conductor using an iron bar for the purpose carried on the car. Basically the line was single, apart from a good ration of passing loops and a long stretch in Swadlincote along two roads away from the double junctions. As mentioned, the gauge was 3 ft. 6 in. to match that of the Burton system.

Burton-on-Trent supplied the current as far as the borough boundary and there was no difficulty in matching the supply to that provided by the B & A. A track booster was, however, required for the longer Ashby section.

Overhead wiring was supported by poles with single brackets or poles with span wires round curves. There was at least one double bracket at the foot of the bridge in Swadlincote where the depot line emerged. The height of the posts was 31 ft. and maximum bracket length 16 ft. Where an impression was to be made posts had ornamental cast bases with the MR coat of arms on them, as well as wrought iron scrollwork above, otherwise they were plain. The wire hangers were the usual curved 'eyebrow' shape, with some plainer, straighter ones here and there for variety. The line was laid with two parallel wires above it throughout, one for each direction of running which did away with the need for points at passing loops. On each car the trolley boom was sited towards the centre of the roadway, that is somewhat off-centre in each car, thus this varied at times, depending on which way round the car had been set to run. The trolley booms could be retrieved by a cord attached.

On one occasion a trolley arm left the wire and swung into the roof of a shop in High street, Swadlincote, dislodging some tiles. The shopkeeper complained, there was a dispute and the tram in question was taken in due course round, but did not reach as far as the roof. This was obviously an astute way of evading one's liability, as someone realised that, if the tram were running the other way round, as the trolley equipment was offset on the floor of the upper deck, then it was unlikely to have the same reach as before.

An ingenious device was a signalling system at places where the single line section was long between passing places and not wholly visible to a waiting car. On the last convenient post before the section began up to three lights could be illuminated to denote the number of cars approaching 'In section'. The device was worked by the wheel on the trolley arm passing over a skate on the wire at either end of the section. Difficulties might probably arise when large convoys of Sunday school children, using up to six vehicles were on the move together-presumably they had to run together in groups of three. The most pointwork occurred in the depot and at the main junctions in Swadlincote and Gresley. I am reminded of my early days spent living with the Doncaster trolley bus system which used just five points in the town to run 36 vehicles on seven routes. Transfers from route to route were done by deft manipulation of the bamboo poles with hooks to reconnect the vehicle with the overhead, after it had been manhandled correctly underneath. However, the running points were changed by skate on the overhead wire; the Burton & Ashby system probably used a manual system worked by a stirrup handle on the post.

The depot was just north of the railway at Swadlincote, adjacent to the road bridge and on railway land next to goods depot. Its dimensions were 92 ft. long by 72 ft. width, with eight roads each able to hold three cars which was ample for the 20 which actually arrived. Two of the lines extended to the rear into paint and repair shops, while there were also ticket and timekeeping offices, a messroom and lavatories.

An overhead repair tower wagon was used, drawn by an MR horse based at Swadlincote goods depot. The vehicle had road wheels and was thus unsuitable for the reserved sections of track where a tram had to be used, the men working off a structure on the upper deck.

The powers station was adjacent to the depot and the railway yard; one might also state that it was adjacent to a small colliery which would have yielded a regular supply of cheap fuel in its backyard. In its wisdom, however, the company decided to use the new idea of diesel engines for generating electricity, which were supplied by the Diesel Engine Company of Ghent, vertical engines, each of three cylinders of $15\frac{1}{2}$ in by 23 in. developing 240 BHP, of 172 revs. per minute. Normally one engine was in use, with the other spare. Generators were six pole, supplied by British Westinghouse and producing 165 kw. at 550 volts. There was a storage battery to provide emergency back-up. The fuel supplied was a petroleum by-product, initially for 54/6d. a ton which arrived in 10 ton tank wagons at the adjacent goods yard and was piped to two round storage holders to hold some five months' supply. At some time during the 1914-18 War a leak developed on one of the diesel engines and spare part was ordered and sent from Belgium. The ship bringing this was, alas, torpedoed and the company had to improvise by patching up until closure followed five years later.

One of the engines had driven the power plant at the 1904 Brussels Exhibition. Here both engines were required when all the cars were in service, though the morning service of five cars could run off the battery which was provided, with one engine being fired up after midday. At first both had open exhausts which gave rise to many local complaints about noise and fumes, surprising in this atmosphere of rare smells, until remedial action was taken by fitting chokes. The actual fracture was due to subsidence in the foundations causing a break to the crankshaft web on No. 2 engine. Derby works fitted a strap round the ailing part and things continued to hop along.

The actual vehicles were of the normal tramway pattern, built at the Brush works in Loughborough. They were finished in Midland livery of crimson lake with gold lining and with the coat of arms on the lower side panels. Top deck panels and the lower boards were in white. In later years the gold ornamentation was modified and after 1923 the off-white was to be found on the upper deck exterior only, while the LMS coat of arms now appeared and the gold lining was even simpler. Electric equipment was two Westinghouse No. 80 motors of 25 hp. driving a Brush rigid wheelbase truck. BTH controllers, magnetic track brakes and hand brakes were fitted, worked by wheel. The length of each car was 27 ft. 6 in., 6 ft. 6 in. wide and 13 ft. 3 in. high, seating 51 passengers, 20 inside and 31 outside. The original description for the opening day gave the

Left. No. 10 outside the depot probably destined for the Coronation of King George V. At the controller is Driver Goodman   *Coll: C. Adcock*

15

figures of 57,22 and 35 respectively, probably an estimate before the product reached the line ex-works. The cars were in two batches, numbered 1-13 and 14-20. Each car arrived in a sort of D.I.Y. kit form with upper deck side panels flat on the upper deck floor and the curved upper ends on the driving platforms. Upper deck seats were of slatted wood and each was fitted with a gabardine apron to keep customers as dry as possible, as well as an anti pick-pocket screen to prevent wandering fingers. Inside below were two longitudinal seats of punched veneer which were marginally superior to the slats, though both of these chafed the backs of the knees of countless little boys. Within the lower saloon there was moulded panelling and ornate glass shades for the lighting arrangements. At first a hooter was used to give warning to other road users, but during the Great War bells were substituted, working in the normal manner by foot pedal and handily placed for treading on as those same little boys came careering down the stairs.

It goes almost without saying that the driver stood and faced the elements, while on Nos. 14-20 the understairs space had its own enclosure for the conductor and parcels in bad weather. A scale of charges for parcels was available: 7lb. 3d. 14lb. 5d. 21lb. 6d. 28lb. 7d. 42lb. 8d. 56lb. 9d. For items of up to 500lb. the Company could be asked to consider the matter; obviously it was little use to turn up at the nearest stop and wait with a grand piano or similar! Personal luggage of up to 28lb. could be carried free of charge.

The Burton-on-Trent cars were 24 in number and also in crimson lake, but built by Dick, Kerr and not Brush. Some were later fitted with covers for the top deck and could be distinguished by the upper deck destination boxes, whereas the B & A cars had these placed just above the driver's head. The destinations were the obvious ones, plus 'Private' and 'Car Sheds'.

Opening day and a run on the line

The line was ready for opening and Major Pringle first inspected the Burton corporation extension on High Bank road, traversing the whole section over which the B & A had running powers from the Town Hall to the boundary, all two miles on 31st. May 1906. From there, however, he went for a spin in a Burton car to Swadlincote, where his progress stopped, as the bridge over the railway was still to be completed. The section from Ashby back to the Burton borough boundary was opened on June 8th. and passed muster in the presence of many railway worthies and, no doubt, plenty of local talent.

Services began between Burton and Swadlincote on 13th. June 1906 and throughout on 2nd. July, while the route from Swadlincote to Gresley opened on 24th September and Woodville to Gresley on 15th. October.

Almost all the activity centred on Swadlincote which was roughly halfway. The line was the only example of a railway-owned tramway running over a municipal system. Other there were, though these kept exclusively to their own lines-the Grimsby & Immingham, Cruden Bay, Sandgate, Wisbech, Wantage and Wolverton, also the Hill of Howth in Ireland. Perhaps the systems most closely similar in flavour, however, were the Notts. & Derbyshire and Mexborough & Swindon tramways which both passed through similar scenery over comparable distances.

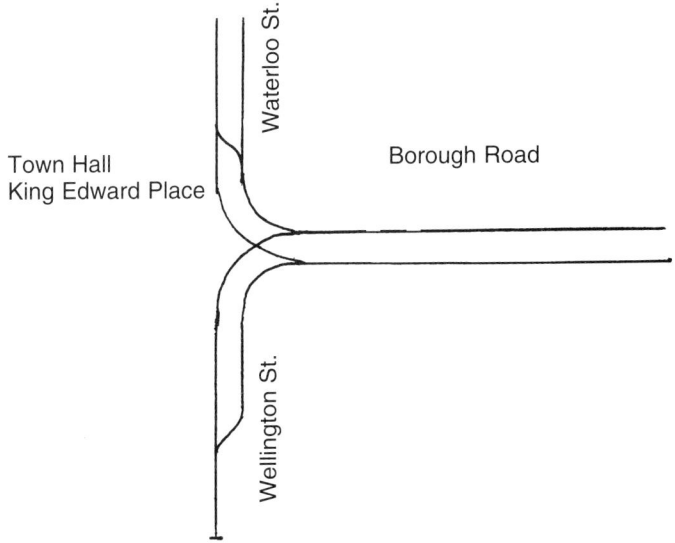

The Burton trams ran along four routes from Station street to Horninglow, Branston road, Stapenhill and Winshill, while the B & A cars enjoyed a little individuality in the town by running along Guild street parallel to High street, more than likely to avoid congestion there at busy times. The B & A service began at a dead-end line round the corner from the Town Hall in Wellington street, from which it then passed across Burton railway station by an overbridge. Here was a busy place with many goods lines flanking the large single island platform to which a wide ramp led down from the main buildings on the bridge. There had been an original station built a short distance away from here up to 1883, but the island pattern was decided upon, possibly proving to be rather difficult to operate but very convenient for passengers. The platform still survives though the building disappeared around 1971.

Over the bridge, then and along Borough road and Station street, then turning north into Guild street which brought the line to a T junction with

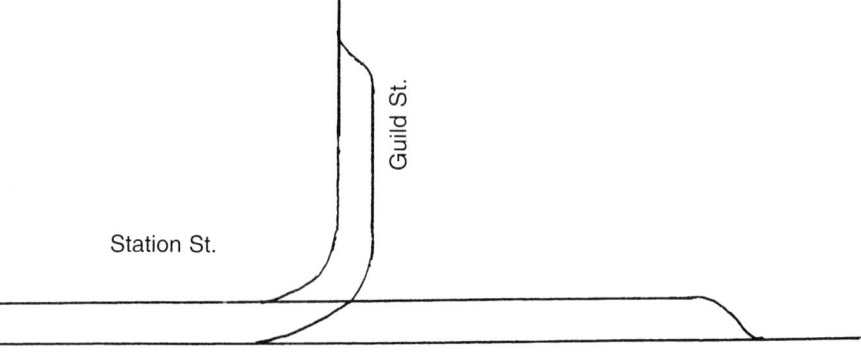

Horninglow street where a right turn was made just in front of the Corporation tram depot opposite. By now the route had passed over four level crossings with brewery lines; no other town was perhaps so greatly enmeshed by such a network, and there were plenty of these appearing from round corners or lurking behind walls complete with fragrant aroma in this back part of town, while the equally fragrant 'Marmite' factory was passed in Station street. along Horninglow street to where the Corporation route came up High street from the south to join the B & A route along Bridge street and then run south east across the Trent Bridge. This was a long affair, since it spanned a division of the river into two. Here were public diversions aplenty, with the municipal baths on the west side and, on the east side to the south by the river, an extended pleasure park with walks, boat houses and band stand. Nor was the land between the two sections of river wasted, as to the north were tennis and bowling greens with yet more boat houses and two cricket grounds, while on the opposite side of the road was another cricket field. The swimming baths were given to the town by the Ratcliffe family and together with other attractions were a good 'draw' for local folk who wished to relax at weekends, perhaps indulging in boating down to Drakelow. A flying meeting held on the Bass meadows nearby brought some 10,000 spectators on one occasion, many of them arriving by tram, for which a passing loop was provided in the centre of the bridge.

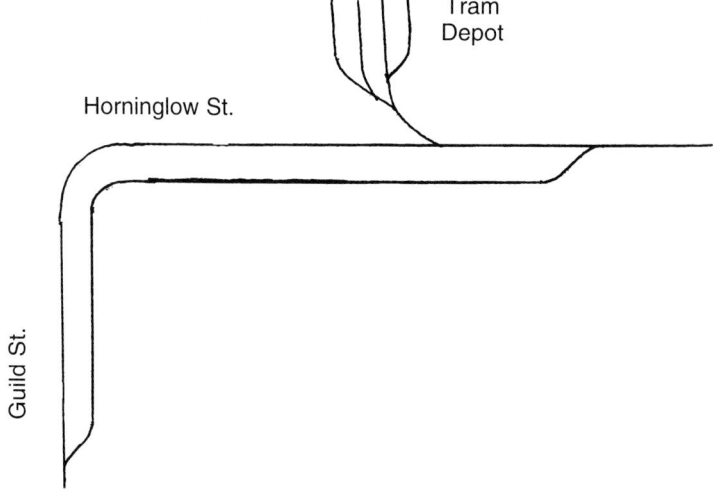

Burton car No. 12 comes round into Station st. Note the high destination indicator and reversed stairs compared with the B&A design

At the end of the bridge and opposite was the Swan Hotel, where the tramway went off north or south, the latter having first of all a passing loop before becoming single, the northern split running as double track along Balmoral road but soon turning east up Bearwood Hill road to form the Winshill route which also carried the B & A cars. The direct Ashby road ran ahead from Trent Bridge and never saw any tram activity. Following the serious tram accident of 1919, mentioned on p.36, the east end of the bridge was widened. There was a passing loop at Mount street which lay on the south side before the tram reached the point, now at 250 ft. (we began at 161 ft.) where High Bank road struck south and for which a double turnout was provided, this continuing as double line up Church hill for a short way and ending in a single line stub by the 'Traveller's Rest'. The line along High Bank road soon became single as far as Alexandra road on the west side, from where a longish run of double track began, running to the point where Ashby road was reached at $\frac{1}{2}$ mile from Trent Bridge direct.

On the north side of the road was High Bank house at 360 ft. and from here it could be said that the line took on its distinctly rural-cum-industrial tone, with passing loops often at sites chosen more for operating convenience than for any idea of accommodating the public. The overhead wires, being double, did not of course need pointwork, though the rail points would be spring where possible to allow passing on the left side. The first loop was near another villa. The First, while the next was at the end of Bretby lane and near a large property, Moat Bank, with a further loop following soon after as the car ran over the country boundary into Derbyshire. The next loop was handily placed outside the clubhouse of Bretby golf course as the line led due south east over the MR colliery branch with its single line and siding to houses, chapel, sawmill and 'Stanhope Arms' on the south side, in front of which was another passing loop at the height of 404 ft.

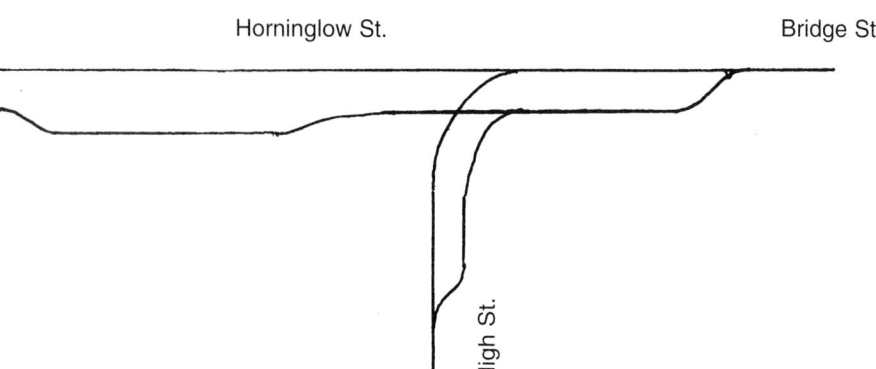

From here it was decided to quit the main road and take in the village of Newhall which had been neglected by the railway earlier. The tramway could have run along Thorntree lane here, but it was decided that this was too narrow and sinuous, and the opportunity was taken to strike away across the field and up to the west side of the village at Sunnyside. Being out of sight of anyone likely to be impressed, the line was furnished with unadorned posts without the swirling wrought ironwork. On Sunnyside was a longer passing loop and it was at each end of this rather unusual 'switchback' section that a light system indicated the occupancy of the line ahead, with up to three cars allowed at any time. This went some way towards relieving embarrassment or confusion in darkness or foggy weather. A skate on the overhead actuated the device. Bretby road was linked by a footpath with the High street beyond as a short cut; this was opened up as a direct run for the tramway to reach the latter thoroughfare and thus provided another section of reserved track, shorter this time, with the footpath fenced off on the north side with the Matsyard colliery and with the first of the two heated waiting shelters provided by the company at the Bretby road end.

Car No. 2 asks everyone to 'Remember the lifeboat demonstration' as it takes the corner at the foot of Bearwood Hill. No. 3 is close behind it as a Burton car goes away uphill.   *National Railway Museum*

The tram now had a fair climb in to the High street, reaching 364 ft. at a further 'Stanhope Arms'. Newhall was an untidy place, though it possessed some sort of centre, with several streets off to the north and a small green, near which was the passing loop, while to the south was the church and market place and, beyond, a good run of decent housing along Parliament street. Along High street the premises of Messrs. Warren, boilermakers were passed, the place where No. 14 was to be restored at a much later date. Where High street became Union road was a further passing loop, while beyond on the south side was the Catholic church and shrine and, opposite, old mine shafts in the field. Shortly the lines executed a right turn into Midland road for the run into Swadlincote, with a passing loop placed on the bend and extending south for a considerable distance. The purpose of siting loops on curves was to give the driver a view into the road ahead, especially if the run-off were uphill, though not so in this case as the road led downhill to the railway bridge over the station, passing firstly one of many potteries in the area, then the sanitary earthernware factory of Messrs. Ault & Tunnicliffe, both on the west side, the latter at the end of the station goods yard. On the east side

21

Winshill Road.   Church Hill.

High Bank Road

lay the tram depot and generator, with eight tracks fanning out from a single line which ran in to the main route as the climb over the railway began. Midland road was left with its original route across the railway by the level crossing. North of the depot was the Shoddy pit, the source of coal which was not made use of when the tramway was put into operation.

Sunnyside, the point where the reserved section ran northwards to Stanhope Bretby. Note the signal lights on the post, one of which is lit as car No. 4 takes the curve   *National Railway Museum*

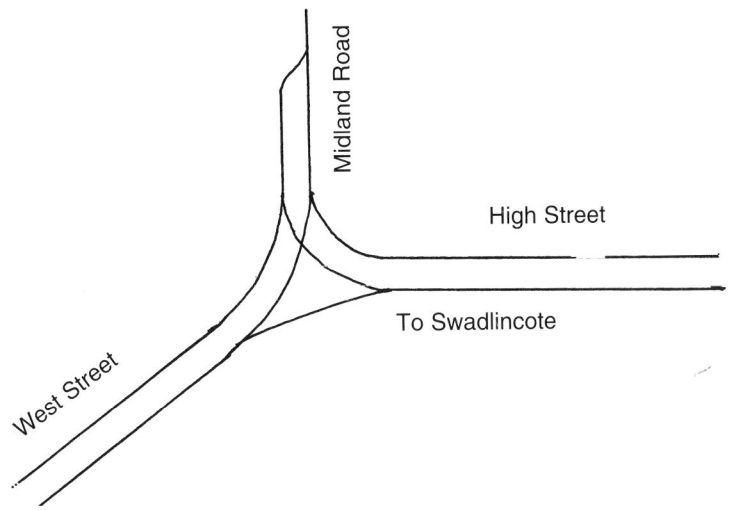

Once off the bridge and the line had a short run past the Town Hall and cattle market on the right, to reach the market place in Swadlincote where was the heart of this small but active system. The height here is 328 ft. This one time market area is also known as the Delph, where an awning of glass and iron ran along the length of the market hall side for waiting passengers to 'shamble' in, and where the building itself was used as a court once a week. The Gresley route ran off here to the south west along West street, and south side of the triangle was formed by a rather odd single line which seemed to be of little direct operational use except to allow a car from the Ashby direction to run into West street, as few, apparently did. Possibly the line was available for turning and standing cars off the Gresley branch.

Into High street then, with the luxury of a track for each direction and with a long pull, sometimes at 1 in 12 for a distance up Hill street over a tunnel carrying a mineral spur from Swadlincote station to a host of potteries, seen as the landscape opens out into a prospect which is reminiscent of Dante, especially at night. Once 400 ft. is gained, the line became single once more, this above the aforementioned tunnel and with Granville pits on the south side. Further south was the hamlet of Jack i' the Hole with its own pottery. North of the road was a large pottery for salt glazing, producing various classes of ware and pipes, with a tall chimney and 25 circular down draught kilns which now provided a new and unpleasant smell to assail the nostrils of those intrepid upstairs passengers who had perhaps left behind the beery fumes of Burton not so long before.

A little further up the hill and across a tramway now, which conveyed clay to the Hill Top fire brick works, after which came the crossing with Woodhouse street on the south side and Bernard street on the north which marked the start of a run of housing in Woodville. At this intersection the B & A route from Gresley came in at a passing place where

Turning round from the view on a previous page, one could see the line becoming single again along the Matsyard section up to Newhall. Note the signalling, skate in the overhead wiring, the wrought ironwork and, lastly, the waiting shed. *National Railway Museum*

a handy mission room was sited at the roadside. As the main route ran east, the scenery became more urban once more with houses on both sides and a passing loop en route until the main Burton-Ashby road, left a long way back, was reached at the old Toll Gate, where five ways converged. Here Hartshorne road ran on ahead, with Moira road opposite. The tram route turned right southwards into High street, with a passing loop on the curve and the other heated waiting shelter provided at the side of the toll building. The police station was also placed here on the opposite side of the road, just to keep an eye on matters. To the west of this important road intersection the Woodville railway goods branch had arrived from the south west, passing beneath two of the roads by bridges to reach the goods depot and the Excelsior pottery. Potteries, as expected,

Early in the nineteenth century, when the population of Ashby stood at 4,400, the town had ideas (above its station if the pun is apt) of becoming a spa town such as Bath or Leamington. There were no waters readily available, but these could be transported from a mine at Moira, a nondescript village nearby, where they had been discovered as was often the case when prospectors were at work looking for minerals. A new Ivanhoe Baths building was constructed behind an equally new Hastings hotel, now the Royal, opened in 1822. Other buildings in the Rawdon and Ivanhoe terraces followed for the accommodation of visitors. The railway came in 1849, bringing in people from towns such as Leicester. These were prosperous times; however eventual decline set in and the baths closed in 1884, leaving the elegant buildings to moulder on until their end came in 1962. The Burton & Ashby Light Railway thus played no part in the spa aspect of Ashby's history and it was the railway which greatly increased the town's population to around 7,000 in 1900, while visitors, having battled through the pages of Sir Walter Scott's 'Ivanhoe' of 1820 would come to see the castle and jousting grounds. Today the population of Ashby is some 12,000.

. . . And what of the 'Zouch' connection? The town has been called Ashby-de-la-Zouch since 1160 after Alain, first Lord of the Manor and was probably kept going to avoid confusion between other Ashbys elsewhere.

Car No.3 running in Bath Street Ashby. Visible is a lady pedalling a handsome tricycle

The branch to Gresley

The Gresley branch pursued a more sedate course through a mainly residential district, leaving Swadlincote market place along West street running south west and then turning due south into Alexandra road. At the turn was a large pottery placed, as it were, to send passengers off on their jaunt uphill along a straight road with double tracks as far as the library on the east side. The single line was resumed at Stanhope road and led into Church avenue past Holy Trinity and then south east into Wilmot road as far as Gresley common, where the line then neatly struck off across the corner on to a short reserved section furnished with a passing loop. Its course then took it to York road for a short distance, after which it turned south again into Market street. Affairs were well laid out here, with grass and trees planted following an earlier period when small shallow pits were dug here by individuals who would mine coal for themselves and local use. The atmosphere was quite a contrast to the main route in general. Curving round Market street in order to run more westerly, the line reached Common road, down which the shortlived branch from Woodville had come, joining it at a passing loop near the 'Boot' inn where there was room to spread out the track and wires somewhat with the attendant pointwork. To the left there had been the old local lock-up building which was later given a chinmey and turned into the premises of the council refuse destructor, possibly a good case of maintaining the site for similar use!

The bulk of Church Gresley was now to the north of the line with evidence of industry revealing itself to the south. There was a further passing loop at the end of Queen street. The car next reached St. George's square, which it crossed, passing one of the most interesting parts of the run, for here was the church of St. George and St. Mary, originally two churches which occupy the same site, the first being the parish church, the second a much older priory foundation. The present building is unusual in that the chancel and tower are both at the east end. Most interesting of all, perhaps, was that Church Gresley colliery, with all its smoke and bustle, lay close behind the church on its hill, while across the road was the sanitary earthenware premises of Church pottery. Here, then, would be a good living for a tramway loving, coal-burning clergyman with a bent for clay-modelling!

On due west now to the top of Cappy Hill at 320 ft. with a passing loop on the curve where a notice requested descending cars to stop and ascending cars to stop on request. The bottom was swiftly reached with a passing loop at 270 ft. and the line ran on westwards alongside the station to end beyond it just north of the road overbridge. Waiting cars would most likely stand in the previous loop, as the dead-end was simply the single line. This was now Castle Gresley: there were earthworks a little further on from the station which was known as Gresley and from where a line went south to Netherseal colliery. South of the station was the small villiage of High Cross Bank.

A happy throng off for the day from Church Gresley, with a few possible cases of overloading, one might think. The leading driver is in civvies

The Woodville to Gresley branch tram line, which had a life of only six years, was a short one which ran south west along Woodhouse street at Woodville from its junction with the main line and into Common road, passing over four tramways and between Granville Nos. 1 and 2 pits en route. There was one passing loop at Coppice side, along which road were the nearest accessible houses, otherwise the purpose of the line was indeed to serve workers in this industrial district, as well as some Sunday school traffic.

B & A operation and services

The resident Engineer and Manager was Mr. James Toulmin, with office at Swadlincote and home by the station approach at Ashby. The opening of the B & A was expected on 31st. May 1906, but was delayed for a time as the machinery at the power station had not been sufficiently tested, nor were the staff completely au fait with matters. Eventually, however, Mr. Toulmin was able to send a wire to Derby on 2nd. July at 3.55 p.m.: 'Opened for traffic successfully this morning.' There was no formal junketing, merely a letter of congratulation from Head Office, though events caused a great deal of interest among the local population as shown by the numbers present in old photographs of the first car, No. 13

29

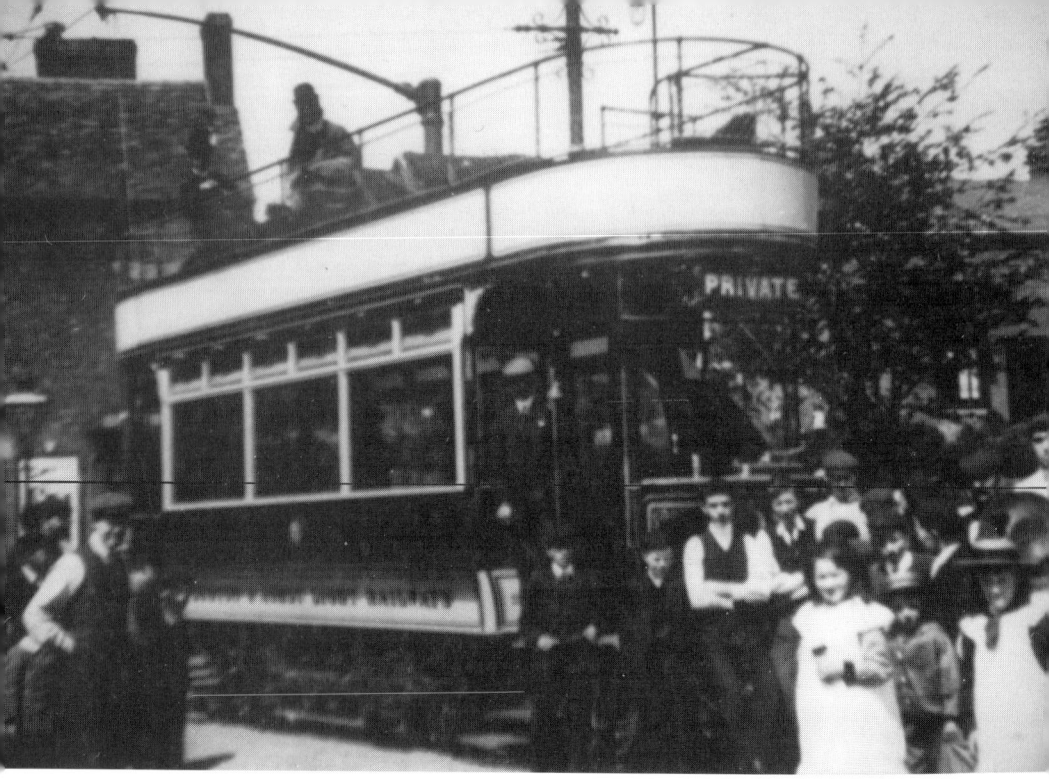

Anonymous car with admirers standing apparently in High Bank Road Winshill. According to the overhead, the car is standing on the Burton Corporation section beyond the junction leading to the Winshill terminus.

1906, with the Woodville-Gresley line following on 15th. October. At first there was a half hourly service of trams on all three routes and cars started at the same time from each end of the main route. The odd man out, that is the route between Woodville and Gresley, soon became hourly using a single car, then Saturdays Only, closing in November 1912.

The two surviving lines were profitable until after the end of the Great War, with over three million passengers carried each year. Like the railways, the cars carried a great deal of Sunday school traffic at this time, golden days when hosts of neatly dressed children were taken out at local beauty spots situated not too far away from base. One of these was Brizlincote, seat of the Earl of Caernarvon, while Bretby village was popular. There were of course Ashby Bath grounds and the castle. Gresley especially was a good source of customers for such diversions, and quite often up to six cars would be employed at a time to turn out at weekends.

In 1919 clouds began to form on the horizon; the income per car mile of 1/11d. did not sit easily next to the outgoing of 2/4 d. A loss of £5,543 was incurred in that year. The old palliative was introduced first of all, when advertising appeared on cars. At this distance in time it seemed to enhance the interest of the vehicles in the photographer's eye - what exactly was 'Nubolic'?

At the Grouping of the railways in 1923 the revenue per car mile was now 1/10 d set against expenditure of 1/1 d, a difference of 9d as against 5d before. Traffic fell, partly due to men who had left the forces setting up in business on their own account to compete with their own ex-army vehicles. The number of passengers carried fell to two million yearly by 1924, then to 1½ million as the road competition began to bite. The crunch came with the General Strike of 1926 which closed several tenuous country and branch workings on the railways.

The through fare had been 6 d. in 1906 and 9 d. in 1919; a reduction was tried, but in the final days the fare was 10½ d. Workmen's fares were applied before 8 a.m. and after 5 p.m. at a rate of ½ d per mile, giving a 10 d. fare for the ten miles run from end to end. In London, Midland & Scottish railway days, when all fare stages seem to have arrived in odd halfpennies, a 5½ d ticket was white with a yellow stripe. At first the 6d. ticket was blue, while the lower values were a 1 d. white and 1½ d orange. The issues were all Williamson type with each stage printed on for punching as required:-

Wellington Street	Corporation Tram Depot
Swan Hotel	Alexandra Road
Bretby Lane	Stanhope Bretby
Sunnyside Newhall	Hope & Anchor
Swadlincote Market Place	Boot Inn Gresley
Woodhouse Road Jc.	Station Street, Woodville
Woodville Reservoir	Boundary Chapel
Malt Shovel, Annswell	Golf Links, Ashby
Hill Street Loop, Ashby	Ashby Station
Rising Sun, Gresley	Gresley Station

Each ticket was thus a microcosm of the whole system, bettered only by the older German idea of printing a system map on each ticket and punching the stops at the actual places thereon.

Between 1908 and about 1916 a ten minute frequency had been tried at peak times between Burton and Swadlincote, occupying some 17 cars at the time. Additional cars were put on between Burton and Woodville after 1922, from 2.20 to 8.20 p.m., the last car leaving Woodville at 9.22 p.m., while the through service now commenced at 8 a.m. from each end. A 40 minute interval was run with the last car leaving Burton at 9.40 p.m. to Woodville and Ashby at 10.20 p.m. to Swadlincote. The cars from Gresley always connected with the main route services at Swadlincote.

The car sheds at Swadlincote. Visible are Nos. 18, 5, 14 and 9. No. 1 stands outside with the power station behind   National Railway Museum

On Saturdays a 20 minute service was tried, with a 10 minute frequency in the evenings between Burton, Sunnyside, Newhall and Woodville. On the Gresley line the later frequency was also 40 minutes with the first car at 6.15 a.m. from Swadlincote running to Gresley colliery, while on Saturdays there was a 20 min service in the afternoons. The last tram left Gresley station at 10.48 p.m. The colliery working ran from Swadlincote Market Place to Boundary Chapel, then back to Swadlincote and over the single line connection on to the Gresley route in Market Place, to the colliery and returning to Swadlincote, then running to Burton, thus turning itself round in the process and evening out the wear on the wheels.

And what of Sundays? Between Burton and Ashby cars ran every 40 minutes between 2.00 and 8.40 p.m. and Burton-Woodville every 40 minutes between 2.20 and 9.20 p.m. On the branch, services ran every 40 minutes between Swadlincote and Gresley from 1.28 to 10.08 p.m., the car waiting 12 minutes at Swadlincote to connect. The last timetable offered a reasonable service at 20-30 minutes' frequency between Burton and Swadlincote, these extended to Woodville on Saturdays. There were eleven weekday trips between Burton and Ashby, the car to Burton leaving ten minutes before the car to Ashby, both passing at Stanhope Arms Newhall or Darklands road. The Gresley service was

Cars No.1 and 13 of the first batch wait outside Ashby station at the start of what is more than likely a Sunday school treat. No sign of the crews, but there seems to be a railwayman on the extreme right.

Coll: C.T. Goode

reduced, with an early car leaving Swadlincote at 7.47 a.m., then nothing until 5.08 p.m. and seven trips until the last run at 10.08 p.m. The Saturday services, however, remained at 20-30 minutes interval during the day.

Revenue had continued to fall, however, from a weekly £520 in 1924 to £338 in 1925 and a paltry £88 in 1926. Single manning of cars had been considered but refused by the Board of Trade as the cars did not lend themselves to it. With some regret, therefore, and not a little relief, a system which had in fact competed with its close cousin, the railway within its own family, and with the newfangled mode of transport, the bus, lowered the booms for the last time when the last cars had run on 19th. February 1927.

The staff

The staff were almost all local men, with some ladies during the wartime period and afterwards. The first drivers were from Burton engine shed, chiefly fireman awaiting promotion to drivers. Like all small and original systems, they developed a fierce local pride in the operation and upkeep of the cars and services, adding a patina of liveliness and efficiency to an industrial area which needed it. The clanging of the bell, swishing of the trolley wheel, deep drone of the motors on moving off and ringing of the wheels as they took the curves would all be part of the scene, along with the banter between conductor and passengers who would certainly know each other. Such delights are missing from the photographs which exist. On Sundays the drivers wore white tops to their hats and white gloves for a time, as can be detected on occasional views of outings, though at least one shows someone driving in civvies. The apocryphal story exists of two cars meeting on the single line, one of them loaded with jovial, inebriated miners in the best D. H. Lawrence tradition, with neither car willing to give way. Things would, one feels, be run too well for this sort of thing to occur. Two staff photos. exist, one taken at the beginning of things, the other at the very end, with a background at the depot of dull and weary cars. The names of staff where known, were given below both, and the lists are printed below; it is worthwhile studying to see how many names survived the course of the B & A's all too brief history:

Opening Day. Total staff 59, including unknown.

. . Clipson - Driver
Joe Rice - Cleaner
Sam Hickson - Fitter
Albert Hickson - Yardman
Horace Pearce - P. W. Foreman
. . Walton - Conductor
Chris Wells - Driver
Harry Bark - conductor/Driver
William Jinks - Driver
James Stone - Inspector
Robt. Brown - Driver
Jack Winfindale - Conductor

Joe. Pickering - Inspector
Bob. Brown - Driver
. . Winfindale - Conductor
. . Coates - Inspector
Freddy Goodman - Office Boy+
'Tiny' Shaw - ?
. . Baldwin - Traffic Supt.
. . Tunnicliff - Junior Clerk
Richard Shipton - Conductor/Driver

. . Turner - Fitter
George Clamp - Yardman
Jerry Bonner - Controller/Cleaner
. . Williams - Brakesman
. . Tidmarsh - Cleaner
William Lilley - Lineman*
Harrison - ?
Freddie Fox - Driver
. . Woodhall - Inspector
James Jeffs - Driver
Tom. Marsden - Conductor
Arnold Marlborough - Conductor/Driver
Joe Newbald - ?
Len. Hopkins - Conductor/Driver
Fred Redfern - Conductor/Driver
. . Beck - Ticket Clerk
. . Gardner - Shed Foreman
James Toulmin - Manager
William Barton - Cashier
. . Webster - Inspector
. . Pearce - ?
C. Insley - ?

* later became Chief Engineer, + later became Chief Cashier

Staff on Closure in 1927. Not likely to be a complete list.

George Fish	Harold Goodman	Albert Walker
Fred. Parnham	H. Gibson	John Dawkins
Reg. Hart	William Redfern	William Lilley
Edgar Thackwell	Alfred Dakin	James Toulmin (Man.)
Walter Smith	Joseph Newbold	William Barton (Ass. Man.)
H. Shakespeare	James Jeffs	Fred. Goodman (Cashier)
Jack Hickson	J. Pickering	J. C. Armstrong
William Morton	R. W. Jinks	C. Flowers
W. H. Roberts	Thos. Astle	Fred Young
R. Harrison	Robert. H. Brown	B. H. Wileman
Vicotr Norgate	James Salt	George Tomlinson
Richard Shipton	B. H. Wileman	R. C. Lilley

Car No.9 climbs up High Bank Road Winshill to join the Ashby Road.

Trials and Tribulations

Accidents on the line were fortunately infrequent; the maximum speed of the cars was officially no more than 18 mph. in any event. However, there were two incidents, the first, kindly mentioned by Mr. K. Hillier, appeared in the 'Burton Observer' of 14th. June 1906 and must have been the earliest recorded event:-

Bicycle Accident

'A young man named Flint, of Breedon, was thrown from a bicycle and injured whilst riding down Ingles Hill on Saturday night (9th.) owing, it is stated, to his wheel being caught in the tramline on the newly laid Burton & Ashby Light Railway. He was conveyed home in a trap.'

Mr. Hillier mentions the Ashby Show, held in July and August of 1925 to 1928 on Ingles Hill, and states that the light railway conveyed hundreds to the adjacent stop in the last two years of its existence, right by the gates.

The other incident was a much more serious affair and took place when car No. 19 ran back down Bearwood Hill:-

'Through the overturning of a Burton & Ashby Light Railway car at the foot of Bearwood Hill, Winshill on Wednesday, 8th. October last, one person was killed and more than twenty injured, several of these being of a serious nature. The surprising feature of the case was that it was a car ascending and not descending the hill which ran away, the brakes failing to arrest the vehicle

'The incident took place at 11.35 a.m. at 170 yd. from the bottom of the hill. Driver Insley operated the sanding gear and applied the brakes. The conductress Lilian Parker was collecting fares on the top deck. She rushed to the rear platform and clung to the handbrake, the car overturned and shot 15 passengers over a hedge into the garden of River House. One woman, Caroline Hughes, died of her injuries on reaching hospital. Nine were allowed home after treatment and six were detained in hospital. The conductress had severe leg injuries, being pinned under the car. Assistance was rendered by car-jacks, police, a runner, pointsman, coalman, corporation labourer, painter and a cobbler with a dummy leg. The houseowner and her daughter found people staggering about in the drive and the gate smashed by the derailed car. The latter got out a boat and rowed to Dickenson's boathouse where she borrowed a bike to fetch her father, Mr. Hughes the chemist.'

'The driver was in shock, but gave no heed to himself until after the unfortunate conductress had been released from the wreckage. She died six days later in hospital, following the amputation of a leg. The car was righted by horse power on the day following the accident, placed back on the rails and, to the surprise of everyone was driven to Swadlincote by its own power.'

No. 14 being towed along, unmistakably across the water if the motive power is anything to go by
Coll: C.T. Goode

This account appeared in the Burton Observer on 11th. October, 1919.

Repairs were carried out to the car in the Derby Carriage & Wagon Works and it was returned to service in due course. It was rumoured that the women cleaners at the depot were reluctant to work on No. 19 after these sad happenings.

The cars could have been fitted with the Pringle Emergency Brake, in addition to the usual safeguards, and no reason for the run-back and failure to stop appears to have been recorded. The Pringle idea was conceived by Mr. P. J. Pringle, Manager of Burton-on-Trent tramways who devised a track brake shoe placed in front of each rear wheel for each direction of running, so that when applied, the rear wheels rode up partly on to each shoe which thus acted like a sort of chock. A Burton car was fitted and tests were made on 6th. and 9th April 1908 on Hill street Swadlincote on the 1 in 12 rise. Runs were made at various speeds, including one at 34 mph. in wet weather, when the car stopped in 125 ft. Tests were made on the level on Ashby road and on the 1 in 70 of High Bank road. Six Burton cars were subsequently fitted, though it is not clear which B & A cars had the privilege. Given the method of actuation, one wonders if the appliance would work in the event of a run-back.

Mr. Goodman states that the Pringle Brake was not actually fitted to any B & A car, so this device was not in any way to blame for any failure. Being October, there were leaves about and the wheels had begun to slip on these; the magnetic brake lever was pulled round to the brake position, though the reversing lever had not been reversed. New, large type magnetic brakes had been fitted to work on the rails only, which replaced the original wheel block brakes and two small rail shoes.

The LMS company had financial connections with Midland Red buses and could substitute petrol vehicles with a clear conscience on a route from Burton to Ashby roughly along the same roads as the tramway. A route went to Woodville via Newhall and Swadlincote and another to Gresley station via the same places. Parkes Motors had a garage near the town depot in Swadlincote and ran between Burton and Ashby with an alternative route via Stapenhill. They also went to Measham via Swadlincote and Gresley and to Linton, which lay just south of Gresley station beyond High Cross Bank. Thus the wider range and flexibility of the bus was displayed; every one was under cover and works services could be operated as required. Regent Motors did run particular services between Burton and Gresley colliery at this time.

Car No. 5 heads downhill for Swadlincote

Thereafter life changed along with the times as new buildings appeared to replace the old, roads were widened and the old was swept away and largely forgotten. It is hard to imagine today where the light railway ran. After the accident the Trent bridge at Burton was widened at the eastern end, and in 1982 the old Ivanhoe Baths in Ashby were demolished. The road bridge at Swadlincote exists as an access point for the Midland Red bus garage, and British Coal workshops are on the site of the old tram depot, perhaps a neat little irony. Ashby station still retains the bulk of its Greek facade, minus the toplights, and is occupied by an insurance company. These remarks are of course at the time of writing; anything can quickly change. Up to about 1977 there were still tramlines left in the setts of the station approach, visible until the developer who bought the site hid them beneath the garden walls of the desirable residence constructed on the site. The author now understands that a section of retrieved line is presently in the town museum at Ashby. Nobody was brave or foolhardy enough to rescue one of the roadside poles supporting the overhead wiring, but at least one is believed to survive at Sunnyside, Newhall (O/S Ref: 286122) complete with MR emblem.

Ten of the cars were sold off to the Tynemouth & District Electric Traction Company, and it is believed that six of them ran there for a time. The remainder took retirement as sundry pavilions, sheds and greenhouses locally. Mr. Solomon Whitaker of Church Gresley bought Nos. 6, 14 and 15 for that purpose, from where No. 14 was to rise phoenix-like when it was discovered by a preservation group and partially restored at a local boiler foundry. Mr. John Woodman of the Blackpool Trolleycar Co. Ltd. of New York offered welcome assistance in his willingness to aid completion and to have the car running in the USA. Things began to happen in May 1980 when the car was shipped out to Detroit after reaching an acceptable form, there to be fitted with an ex Portuguese Brill truck and painted accurately in the second MR style. No. 14's debut was at the Republican Congress, sponsored by Michigan Bell Telephones, making a corner 'that was forever England', at least until the operating lease ran out.

Train services on major local railways

The earliest source available for details of railway services on the Swadlincote line is dated July 1883, when the corner of a page in 'Bradshaw' devoted little more than the size of a postage stamp to the 'Swadlincote and Woodville branch' and stated that trains were from Burton at 9.22 a.m., 12.48 p.m., 3.10 SO and 6.15. Trains left Woodville at 8.05 and 11.15 a.m., 3.50 p.m. SO and 6.50, all stopping at Swadlincote. In the following years matters deteriorated even further, with a single line of print stating that trains left Burton for Swadlincote at 11 a.m. and 6 p.m., leaving Swadlincote at 7.15 a.m. and 12.05 p.m., with no mention of Woodville.

The essence of it all. Car No. 11 comes past the Royal Hotel in Ashby on a Sunday working - the driver has a white top to his hat. In the background is the large board advertising the station, while a horse trough is seen on the right.
National Railway Museum

By 1910 the loop, as it had by then become, had six daily trains from Burton, most of them going forward to Ashby.

In 1914 the service round the loop had probably reached its most effective form:

Burton	dep:	6.40 am	10.10	1.13 pm	5.05	6.40
Swadlincote	arr:	6.55	10.24	1.28	5.14	6.52
Woodville	arr:	7.03	10.31	1.33	5.20	6.57
Ashby	arr:	7.21	10.53	1.50	5.40	7.16
Coalville	arr:		11.07			
Leicester	arr:		11.50			
Coalville	dep:	8.00 am				
Ashby	arr:	8.11	1.35 pm	3.54	7.45	
Woodville	arr:	8.30	1.52	4.12	8.03	
Swadlincote	arr:	8.37	1.58	4.17	8.09	
Burton	arr:	8.50	2.08	4.30	8.20	

The run was quicker than the light railway at about 36 minutes, but infrequent. There were no Sunday trains. There were 7-9 trains at Gresley, on the Burton-Leicester direct line, and two each way on Sundays. The direct run between Burton and Ashby took 20 minutes.

After the formation of the LMS in 1923, the train service was as follows:

Burton	dep:	7.07 am	11.05	5.13
Swadlincote	arr:	7.15	11.17	5.26
Woodville	arr:	7.24	11.26	5.35
Ashby	arr:	7.47	11.45	5.54
Leicester	arr:	8.37	12.35 pm	

Leicester	dep:		12.30 pm
Ashby	dep:	8.08 am*	1.22
Woodville	arr:	8.30	1.40
Swadlincote	arr:	8.35	1.45
Burton	arr:	8.46	1.57

* starts at Coalville Town. Again, there were no Sunday trains and no competition with the trams. There were 6-7 trains at Gresley station, with trains on Sundays.

During the 1939-45 war, just one train ran each way round the loop:-

Burton	dep:	7.30 am	Leicester	dep:	12.28 pm
Swadlincote	arr:	7.49	Ashby	arr:	1.24
Woodville	arr:	7.58	Woodville	arr:	1.42
Ashby	arr:	8.19	Swadlincote	arr:	1.48
Leicester	arr:	9.01	Burton	arr:	2.00

Swadlincote Station from the road bridge looking south west
Photo: Douglas Thompson

This was more than likely a parliamentary measure run nominally to keep the passenger service on the books. However, there were still 6-7 trains calling at Gresley. The passenger service round the loop expired on 6th. October 1947, though there were summer Saturday workings until 8th. September 1962. The last of these was a Desford-Blackpool, while a curiosity of a freight working latterly was a North Staffs. Stoke-Wellingborough goods. Passenger workings between Burton and Leicester via Gresley closed on 7th September 1964.

Of the station buildings, Swadlincote was typical MR in pattern, in the style of the excellently restored version now at Butterley, while Gresley was a larger model but plainer, without the barge boards. Woodville was a small affair; it was Ashby which sported the best architecture, of unique Grecian design in grey stone, with the platform canopy comprising an unusual series of five semicircular corrugated iron hoops supported by six columns and set at right angles to the rails. Happily, good foresight has preserved the main building here, which makes a happy association with the hotel across the way.

The MR line to Derby was an apologetic affair, its platform across the station forecourt at a distance from the main building and the single line threading its way between the backs of property as it went northwards to cross two roads, one of them that to Burton.

In 1914 trains left Ashby for Derby via Melbourne at 8.08 a.m., 11.14, 1.18 p.m., 3.55 and 7.08. Arrival at Ashby from Derby was at 9.21 a.m., 11.07, 3.27, 6.30 and 8.01. The time for the journey was between 40 and 50 minutes. The passenger service ceased on 22nd. September 1930.

The MR operated as service from Ashby to Nuneaton via Moira and Measham, though not all trains covered the whole route, as in 1883:

Ashby dep: 7.40 a.m. 11.28 (to Meas.) 2.15 pm SO (to Meas.) and 6.05.
Ashby arr: 10.07 a.m. 12.20 p.m. SO (from Meas.) 3.07 (from Meas.) and 8.47

From 1890 the LNWR was able to run through to Burton or Ashby by means of new spurs to the MR which markedly increased their interest. In 1914 the following services were on offer:

Down   *
Nuneaton LNW   dep: 9.35 am 12.55 pm   5.30   7.25
Burton (calls Gres.) arr: 10.37   1.48   6.18   8.13
          * from London dep. 10.35. Sets down at Gresley only.

Nuneaton LNW   dep: 1.30 am   6.48   Nuneaton MR dep: 9.05 am 8.20 pm
Ashby   arr: 2.38   7.52   Ashby   arr: 10.12   9.15

Up

Ashby	dep: 7.20am	11.35	3.47pm	Ashby	dep: 6.00
Nuneaton LNW	arr: 8.35	12.35	4.43	Nuneaton MR arr: 7.15	
Burton (calls Gres.)	dep: 8.05am	9.48	2.32pm		
Nuneaton LNW	arr: 9.04	10.28L	3.14B		

L to London arr: 12.30pm. B from Buxton dep: 12.45pm. Neither stops at Gresely.

In 1925 the ex LNWR workings were confined to a rail-motor service between Shackerstone and Loughborough, connecting into the main service between Ashby and Nuneaton Trent Valley (LNW). These trains left Ashby as follows:

7.30 a.m., 9.01*, 11.36, 3.47 p.m. and 6.05**. On Sats. one service still left Burton at 1.32 p.m. and called at Gresley.

* to Nuneaton Abbey St. (MR). ** to Shackerstone only.

Arrivals at Ashby were: 8.50 a.m.x, 10.19x, 2.28 p.m., 7.52SO, 8.29SX, 9.28*.

x from Shackerstone. * from Nuneaton Abbey St.

On Saturdays a service arrived at Buxton from Nuneaton at 8.16 p.m., calling at Gresley. The above services arrived working over what was known as the Ashby & Nuneaton Joint line and were withdrawn on 13th. April 1931, though the lines were retained for goods working until the 1960s. Thereafter, Ashby was left, with Gresley, as the sole passenger railway route between Leicester and Burton.

Services on this line survived until September 1964, with 7-8 trains each way, and two on Sundays. In December 1951, for instance, the departures at Ashby were as follows:

To Burton: 5.37 a.m. (starts Coalville), 7.44, 9.59, 1.10 p.m.SO, 4.07SO, 4.12SX, 5.40, 6.27, 7.25, 10.02. Suns: 10.10 a.m., 9.39 p.m.

To Leicester: 6.31 a.m., 7.35, 8.38, 1.16 p.m., 4.09, 6.26, 8.06SO, 9.18. Suns:7.50 a.m., 9.17 p.m.

Ill-met by Gresley Station

By way of a tailpiece (no pun intended), we return to the MR horse, out with the tower wagon to replace a light bulb on the tramway terminal pole at Gresley station. From his perch the lineman asked the horse driver to come up to him and help with the fitting. This he did, having first secured the wheels and leaving the horse to his meditations. Unfortunately a particularly noisy steam engine rushed through the station, which frightened the nag, causing it to think about returning home swiftly. As the tower was fully extended its top caught the overhead wiring; it turned over and shot the two men down the steep, soft and muddy bank at the roadside. Fortunately they were not injured, though the driver landed face down. After a few days the character of the horse was sent from Derby: 'This horse is frightended of steam'.

The Trolley Reverser

A trolley reverser was tried for a time at the Market Place end of West Street in Swadlincote for the use of cars arriving from Gresley. Here the line was double and a crossover was installed by which a car on reversing would gain the right line for the outward run. For readers not familiar with this interesting device, which saved the conductor a trek round the car with the trolley boom to reconnect it, often in the midst of a busy roadway, an explanation is given.

The arriving car ran up from A to B with the trolley wheel crossing point X which was sprung against it. The car then reversed, the trolley arm and wheel being pushed to run over the spring point X again set for the curve to C where point Y was sprung against it. The trolley arm was now at right angles to the car. As the car took the crossover to the correct running line, the trolley arm began to follow, coming through point Y now in favour over the curve round to the point at D which was sprung against it. Sometimes the overhead points had short stocks hanging down which were moved to change the direction by the action of the trolley arm lifting them as it passed beneath.

The device was thus an intriguing application of simple physics with angles, wires and springs; it was fascinating to watch in action and was in evidence on other systems at terminals in Bradford, Sheffield and London at one time. It allowed drivers to show their expertise by executing swift turn-rounds. It was essential, of course, that the trolley arms were all of the same length and that in the case of cars such as the B & A variety, that they were the right way round with the off-set side nearest to the device, otherwise embarrassing situations might occur!

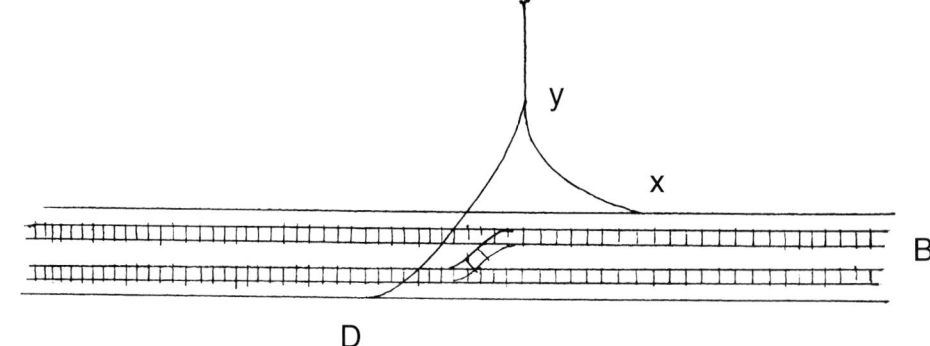

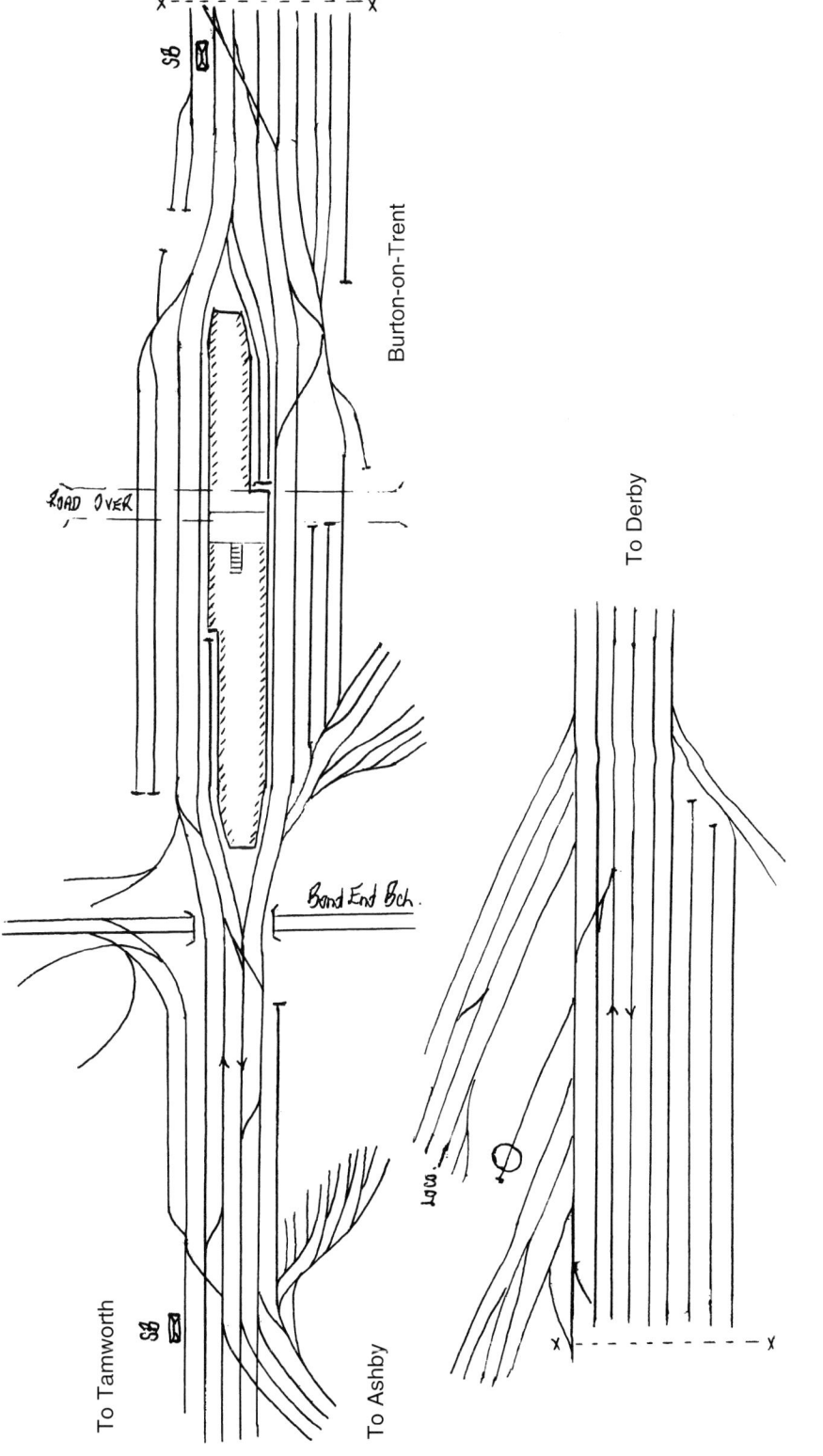

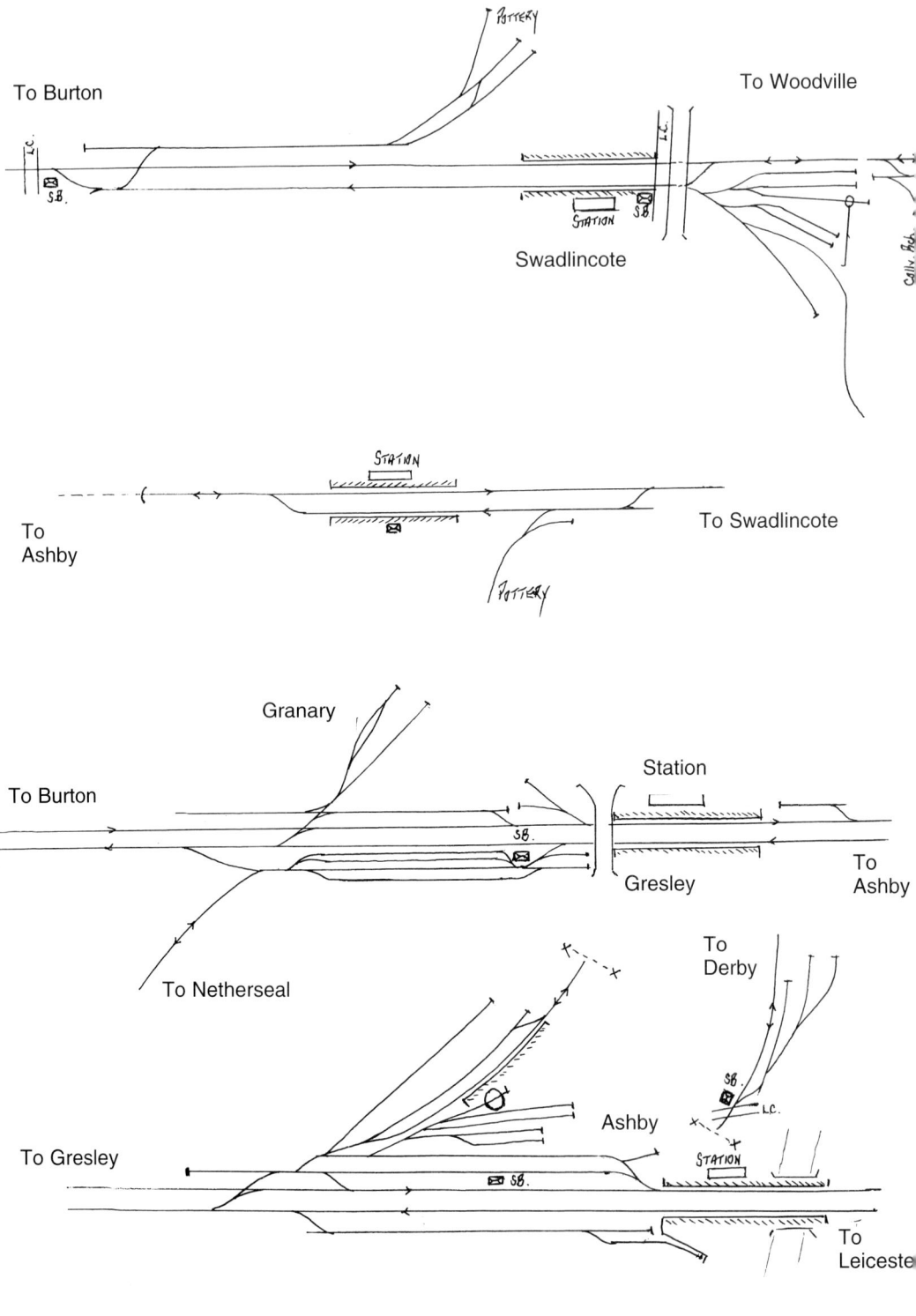

Locomotives at Burton shed (17B). 1961

Class 2P 4-4-0.	40396 (illustrated). 40453.
Ivatt 2-6-2T	41277, 41328.
Brewery 0-4-0T	41532, 41536.
Horwich 2-6-0 Mixed traffic.	42756, 42759, 42163, 42769, 42784, 42799, 42818, 42822, 42824, 42825/6, 42829, 42839, 42847, 42855, 42896/7, 42922.
Johnson 3F 0-6-0	43574, 43608, 43709, 43991.
Fowler 4F 0-6-0	44100, 44124, 44241, 44299, 44332, 44380, 44434-6, 44526/7, 44538, 44541/2, 44551/2, 44562, 44591, 44597/9
Johnson 'Jinty" 0-6-0T	47313, 47458, 47641.

Industrial Premises linked by rail in 1931

Gresley
    Cooper & Harvey's Siding.
    Coton Park Colliery.
    Netherseal Colliery and wharf.

Swadlincote
    Albion Clay Co. Ltd Siding.
    Bretby Brick & Stoneware Co. Siding.
    Bretby Colliery and wharf.
    Cadley Hill Colliery.
    Swadlincote Old Colliery.
    Hawfield Brick & Pipe Works.
    Hearthcote Pottery Co.
    Midland Contractors Supply Co.
    Newhall Field Siding.
    Stanton Colliery. J&N Nadin & Co.
    Stanton House Farm Siding.
    Swadlincote Gas Works Siding.
    Tickler's Heathcote Pottery.
    Woodwards Pipe Works.
    Wragg & Sons Pipe Works.

Woodville
    Albion Clay Co's Siding.
    Donington Pipe & Brick Siding.
    Ensor & Co's Pipe Works.
    Granville Colliery.
    Green & Co's Pipe.
    Hilltop Pottery Co's Siding.
    Jones' Siding.

Knowles & Co's Brick & Sanitary Pipe Works
Mansfield Bros. Tile Works.
Mansfield's Sanitary Sidings.
Mason, Cash & Co's Siding
Church Gresley Colliery.
Moore & Son's Siding.
Outram Pottery Works.
Robinson's Siding.
Tooth & Co's Siding.
Woodville Sanitary Pipe Co's Siding.
Woodward Brick Works.
Wragg & Son's Brick Works.

Other titles by the same Author.

The Railways of Hull.
Railways in South Yorkshire.
The Railways of North Lincolnshire.
The Railways of Castleford.
The Railways of Nottingham.
Huddersfield Branch lines.
The Wakefield, Pontefract & Goole Railway.
The Selby & Driffield Railway.
The Great Northern & Great Eastern Joint Line.
The Dearne Valley Railway.
The Trentham Gardens Branch.